FRANCIS FRITH'S
CLEVELAND LIVING MEMORIES

Dear Mam,

Wishing you a Merry Christmas 2011.

With all our love

Vicky, Steve & Rebecca

xxx

THE FRANCIS FRITH COLLECTION

www.francisfrith.com

FRANCIS FRITH'S

CLEVELAND

LIVING MEMORIES

ROBIN COOK was born in Whitby, North Yorkshire, and has lived for the past 35 years in a small village within the North York Moors National Park. He worked in the chemical industry on Teesside for most of his career, and became involved in local history many years ago. Collecting early books and postcards of the area led him to the publication of eight different hardback volumes of annotated postcards and photographs – mainly from before the First World War – relating to Teesside and the wider Ancient Cleveland area. He is a member of the Cleveland and Teesside Local History Society.

**FRANCIS FRITH'S
PHOTOGRAPHIC MEMORIES**

CLEVELAND
LIVING MEMORIES

ROBIN COOK

First published in the United Kingdom in 2005 by
Frith Book Company Ltd

Hardback Edition 2005
ISBN 1-85937-505-7

Text and Design copyright © Frith Book Company Ltd
Photographs copyright © The Francis Frith Collection

The Frith photographs and the Frith logo are reproduced under licence from Heritage Photographic Resources Ltd, the owners of the Frith archive and trademarks

All rights reserved. No photograph in this publication may be sold to a third party other than in the original form of this publication, or framed for sale to a third party.
No parts of this publication may be reproduced, stored in a retrieval system, or transmitted, in any form, or by any means, electronic, mechanical, photocopying, recording or otherwise, without the prior permission of the publishers and copyright holder.

British Library Cataloguing in Publication Data

Cleveland Living Memories
Robin Cook

Frith Book Company Ltd
Frith's Barn, Teffont,
Salisbury, Wiltshire SP3 5QP
Tel: +44 (0) 1722 716 376
Email: info@francisfrith.co.uk
www.francisfrith.co.uk

Printed and bound in Great Britain

Front Cover: **REDCAR,** *The Beach c1955* R16052t
Frontispiece:**ORMESBY** *c1965* O45037

The colour-tinting is for illustrative purposes only, and is not intended to be historically accurate

Aerial photographs reproduced under licence from Simmons Aerofilms Limited
Historical Ordnance Survey maps reproduced under licence from Homecheck.co.uk

AS WITH ANY HISTORICAL DATABASE THE FRITH ARCHIVE IS CONSTANTLY BEING CORRECTED AND IMPROVED, AND THE PUBLISHERS WOULD WELCOME INFORMATION ON OMISSIONS OR INACCURACIES

CONTENTS

FRANCIS FRITH: VICTORIAN PIONEER	7
CLEVELAND - AN INTRODUCTION	10
MIDDLESBROUGH FROM THE AIR	14
THE MIDDLESBROUGH AND REDCAR AREA	16
SALTBURN BY THE SEA FROM THE AIR	48
SALTBURN AND EAST CLEVELAND	50
STOCKTON ON TEES FROM THE AIR	78
THE STOCKTON AREA	80
HARTLEPOOL FROM THE AIR	100
THE HARTLEPOOL AREA	102
INDEX	115
Free Mounted Print Voucher	119

FRANCIS FRITH
VICTORIAN PIONEER

FRANCIS FRITH, founder of the world-famous photographic archive, was a complex and multi-talented man. A devout Quaker and a highly successful Victorian businessman, he was philosophical by nature and pioneering in outlook.

By 1855 he had already established a wholesale grocery business in Liverpool, and sold it for the astonishing sum of £200,000, which is the equivalent today of over £15,000,000. Now a very rich man, he was able to indulge his passion for travel. As a child he had pored over travel books written by early explorers, and his fancy and imagination had been stirred by family holidays to the sublime mountain regions of Wales and Scotland. 'What lands of spirit-stirring and enriching scenes and places!' he had written. He was to return to these scenes of grandeur in later years to 'recapture the thousands of vivid and tender memories', but with a different purpose. Now in his thirties, and captivated by the new science of photography, Frith set out on a series of pioneering journeys up the Nile and to the Near East that occupied him from 1856 unti 1860.

INTRIGUE AND EXPLORATION

These far-flung journeys were packed with intrigue and adventure. In his life story, written when he was sixty-three, Frith tells of being held captive by bandits, and of fighting 'an awful midnight battle to the very point of surrender with a deadly pack of hungry, wild dogs'. Wearing flowing Arab costume, Frith arrived at Akaba by camel sixty years before Lawrence of Arabia, where he encountered 'desert princes and rival sheikhs, blazing with jewel-hilted swords'.

He was the first photographer to venture beyond the sixth cataract of the Nile. Africa was still the mysterious 'Dark Continent', and Stanley and Livingstone's historic meeting was a decade into the future. The conditions for picture taking confound belief. He laboured for hours in his wicker dark-room in the sweltering heat of the desert, while the volatile chemicals fizzed dangerously in their trays. Back in London he exhibited his photographs and was 'rapturously cheered' by members of the Royal Society. His reputation as a photographer was made overnight.

VENTURE OF A LIFE-TIME

Characteristically, Frith quickly spotted the opportunity to create a new business as a specialist publisher of photographs. He lived in an era of immense and sometimes violent change. For the poor in the early part of Victoria's reign work was exhausting and the hours long, and people had precious little free time to enjoy themselves. Most

people had no transport other than a cart or gig at their disposal, and rarely travelled far beyond the boundaries of their own town or village. However, by the 1870s the railways had threaded their way across the country, and Bank Holidays and half-day Saturdays had been made obligatory by Act of Parliament. All of a sudden the working man and his family were able to enjoy days out and see a little more of the world.

With typical business acumen, Francis Frith foresaw that these new tourists would enjoy having souvenirs to commemorate their days out. In 1860 he married Mary Ann Rosling and set out on a new career: his aim was to photograph every city, town and village in Britain. For the next thirty years he travelled the country by train and by pony and trap, producing fine photographs of seaside resorts and beauty spots that were keenly bought by millions of Victorians. These prints were painstakingly pasted into family albums and pored over during the dark nights of winter, rekindling precious memories of summer excursions.

THE RISE OF FRITH & CO

Frith's studio was soon supplying retail shops all over the country. To meet the demand he gathered about him a small team of photographers, and published the work of independent artist-photographers of the calibre of Roger Fenton and Francis Bedford. In order to gain some understanding of the scale of Frith's business one only has to look at the catalogue issued by Frith & Co in 1886: it runs to some 670 pages, listing not only many thousands of views of the British Isles but also many photographs of most European countries, and China, Japan, the USA and Canada - note the sample page shown on page 9 from the hand-written Frith & Co ledgers recording the pictures. By 1890 Frith had created the greatest specialist photographic publishing company in the world, with over 2,000 sales outlets - more than the combined number that Boots and WH Smith have today! The picture on the nest page shows the Frith & Co display board at Ingleton in the Yorkshire Dales (left of window). Beautifully constructed with a mahogany frame and gilt inserts, it could display up to a dozen local scenes.

POSTCARD BONANZA

The ever-popular holiday postcard we know today took many years to develop. In 1870 the Post Office issued the first plain cards, with a pre-printed stamp on one face. In 1894 they allowed other publishers' cards to be sent through the mail with an attached adhesive halfpenny stamp. Demand grew rapidly, and in 1895 a new size of postcard was permitted called the court card, but there was little room for illustration. In 1899, a year after Frith's death, a new card measuring 5.5 x 3.5 inches became the standard format, but it was not until 1902 that the divided back came into being, so that the address and message could be on one face and a full-size illustration on the other. Frith & Co were in the vanguard of postcard development: Frith's sons Eustace and Cyril continued their father's monumental task, expanding the number of views offered to the public and recording more and more places in Britain, as the coasts and countryside were opened up to mass travel.

Francis Frith had died in 1898 at his villa in Cannes, his great project still growing. The archive he created continued in business for another seventy years. By

1970 it contained over a third of a million pictures showing 7,000 British towns and villages.

FRANCIS FRITH'S LEGACY

Frith's legacy to us today is of immense significance and value, for the magnificent archive of evocative photographs he created provides a unique record of change in the cities, towns and villages throughout Britain over a century and more. Frith and his fellow studio photographers revisited locations many times down the years to update their views, compiling for us an enthralling and colourful pageant of British life and character.

We are fortunate that Frith was dedicated to recording the minutiae of everyday life. For it is this sheer wealth of visual data, the painstaking chronicle of changes in dress, transport, street layouts, buildings, housing, engineering and landscape that captivates us so much today. His remarkable images offer us a powerful link with the past and with the lives of our ancestors.

THE VALUE OF THE ARCHIVE TODAY

Computers have now made it possible for Frith's many thousands of images to be accessed almost instantly. Frith's images are increasingly used as visual resources, by social historians, by researchers into genealogy and ancestry, by architects and town planners, and by teachers involved in local history projects.

In addition, the archive offers every one of us an opportunity to examine the places where we and our families have lived and worked down the years. Highly successful in Frith's own era, the archive is now, a century and more on, entering a new phase of popularity. Historians consider the Francis Frith Collection to be of prime national importance. It is the only archive of its kind remaining in private ownership. Francis Frith's archive is now housed in an historic timber barn in the beautiful village of Teffont in Wiltshire. Its founder would not recognize the archive office as it is today. In place of the many thousands of dusty boxes containing glass plate negatives and an all-pervading odour of photographic chemicals, there are now ranks of computer screens. He would be amazed to watch his images travelling round the world at unimaginable speeds through internet lines.

The archive's future is both bright and exciting. Francis Frith, with his unshakeable belief in making photographs available to the greatest number of people, would undoubtedly approve of what is being done today with his lifetime's work. His photographs depicting our shared past are now bringing pleasure and enlightenment to millions around the world a century and more after his death.

CLEVELAND
AN INTRODUCTION

ONE of the fascinating aspects of the world in which we live is that the rate of change is ever increasing. It took many centuries before man invented the wheel, learnt to cultivate and rotate crops, and discovered how to write and to count. Much later, he discovered astronomy, algebra, physics and medicine. In the last hundred years or so he has learnt about oil, the internal combustion engine, the motor car, jet propulsion, atomic energy, computers, space flight, and DNA. The rate at which our society has developed is both exciting and yet perhaps quite frightening. Human beings are being required to adapt to changing circumstances much faster, or they risk being left behind. Society across the world is seeing casualties as some people drop out.

This book of very attractive Frith photographs of the Cleveland area is a living demonstration of that rate of change. Perhaps we do not quite realise how much change is going on around us, because although it is faster than in centuries past, it is happening gradually but relentlessly day by day. It is only when with the help of these photographs we are reminded how our towns and villages used to look no more than forty or fifty years ago, that we are surprised at how much has been going on around us during our own lifetime.

Buildings have often disappeared, whilst new ones - usually less attractive - have risen up. Traffic levels have changed substantially: the ability to buy motor cars has increased significantly, and there has been a major increase in the number of commercial vehicles, nationally and internationally. The ownership and nature of many shops has changed, and so has the provision of leisure facilities. Our public parks and open spaces have sometimes become more neglected, whilst a number of fine shopping centres have come on to the scene during this period.

In the same way, organisations have changed. This book sets out to portray scenes from the 1950s and 1960s in Cleveland. The Cleveland referred to in this case was actually formed by Act of Government in 1974, and it disappeared again in 1996 as further Local Authority re-organisation took place. Nevertheless, to the contemporary public, the expression is still well understood. Historically, the ancient Cleveland existed for many centuries, and comprised that large area of north-east Yorkshire formerly known as the East and West divisions of the Wapentake of Langbaurgh, reaching from the mouth of the River Tees almost to Whitby, and including the Esk Valley, Guisborough, Stokesley and Yarm, and everything within that boundary. It lay within the North Riding of Yorkshire, until the 20th century saw some of the North Riding taken away into the new Teesside Authority in 1968, and a lot more of it when Cleveland County was formed in 1974, at which point the infant Teesside was abandoned. Correspondingly, County Durham lost parts of its south-eastern area into those new authorities at the same time.

In the same way, society is also changing on a gradual basis, not always for obvious benefit. All the more reason, therefore, why it can be comforting to be reminded through these photographs of where we have come from, and how much we valued what we used to have; now we can see both good and bad in the changes which have occurred, but at the time we did not necessarily realise what was going on.

A good example of such change can be found in the case of Middlesbrough. Since these photographs were taken, a major motorway has been driven through the northern end of the town near the railway station, which required the demolition of the impressive Exchange building, built in 1868. The parish church of St Hilda, consecrated in 1840, was demolished in 1969, and within the last two years the Roman Catholic Cathedral in Sussex Street, built in 1878 and unoccupied for some years, was burnt down by vandals. A significant amount of the terraced housing in the old St Hilda's area, as well as along the length of Cannon Street and elsewhere in the central part of the town, was demolished – it was considered unsuitable housing for modern times. The occupants were subsequently housed in new estates elsewhere, creating significant and detrimental social upheaval.

On the other hand, in this same period major shopping centres with weather-proof avenues and associated car parking have been provided in the town centre to help the public. Other nearby streets no longer allow traffic, in order to keep the

MARSKE BY THE SEA, *Marske Hall c1960* M40031

pedestrians safe. Modern law courts have been provided, and the former Constantine College, which later became Teesside Polytechnic, is now the thriving modern University of Teesside with many thousands of undergraduates. Additional modern municipal buildings have been built alongside the Town Hall to improve the administration of local services.

Stockton on Tees has also undergone significant change since the original publication of these photographs. The High Street has been developed in a number of ways, both in traffic flow and in its buildings. The biggest change was the demolition of 400 yards of the east side of the High Street frontage from Finkle Street to the Castle Theatre. A magnificent and varied facade of buildings, including historic coaching inns and quaint shops, was flattened in 1970 in order to build a brick and concrete indoor market and shopping centre. Today our society and the planners would not allow such extensive and official vandalism to happen, but it did then, and now it is too late. Much more recently another big new shopping centre has been developed, and again there were casualties, notably the Baptist Church in Wellington Street (built in 1902) and the former Register Office (built in the early 1880s) in Nelson Terrace - the latter was originally the offices of the Stockton Union Board of Guardians.

By way of contrast, the riverside area of Stockton has been developed. There are now some interesting bridges, and a full-size model of Captain James Cook's 'Endeavour'. The Tees Barrage opened in late 1994 in order to remove the tidal effect of the river and provide clean water for recreation and events, and a major extension of the University of Durham has been built on the Teesdale site, together with significant new office buildings and business locations in the same part of the Thornaby side of the River Tees. New municipal buildings and swimming baths have also been developed in the Church Road area, and some of the older housing estates have been re-furbished with major investments.

In the case of Hartlepool, the town has been completely re-developed since the Frith photographs were taken. A number of the interesting old buildings have survived, although some of the most characterful shopping streets have gone - Lynn Street, for example. However, most people would agree that several major developments in Hartlepool have transformed the town, giving it a new pride and vibrancy. These include the Historic Quay, the Marina, the historic ship re-building programme, the new Museum of Hartlepool, the conversion of Christ Church to the new Art Gallery, and the major covered shopping centre opposite the Civic Centre. There is certainly plenty to see now in what was the former docklands area, but the old Headland neighbourhood also remains quite an intriguing place both for the historian and even for the ornithologist!

Redcar has had to adjust to the significant changes during this same period in the kind of holidays people like to take. Many people now choose to travel abroad, where the warm weather is perhaps more reliable, and the expense involved may not be very much different from a holiday in the United Kingdom. Redcar is not the only resort facing this problem, but it has not been an easy adjustment. Some limited re-development has occurred along the sea front, and a big new shopping centre has recently opened off the High Street. There are plans for further new leisure facilities at the Coatham end of the town, but these will take time to emerge.

The period since the 1950s and 1960s has had its successes and excitements, as well as its disappointments, but they all serve to illustrate just how much has been happening in our lives locally which affects us in our day to day activities. That is why the chance to take time out and look quietly and thoughtfully at the photographs which follow can be a way of measuring the extent of some of those changes. We hope that it will be a re-assuring experience rather than one of concern or sadness!

The smaller towns and villages covered in this selection have also faced the pressure of changes in society during this period, and a number of influences have played a part in their fortunes. The final collapse of the ironstone mining industry in East Cleveland led to many economic uncertainties, and some of the enterprises which were set up subsequently to provide local employment proved to be fragile. Many of the visible relics of the ironstone mining activities have already disappeared, and the younger generation now know little about it, including the significant physical hardships it involved. We may be thankful that the Tom Leonard Mining Museum at Skinningrove has been established to ensure that we do not forget this proud past on which the economics of much of modern Teesside was originally founded.

Cleveland as a local government administrative area lasted a little over twenty years. It was not the easiest organisation to run, because these individual communities all had their own unique and different histories, their own priorities and objectives. But we still talk about it as a concept, because we all got so used to it in the 1970s and 1980s, and into the 1990s. That is why this selection covering that area still seems a natural one to make; this selection also embraces a very interesting mix of different towns and villages, which makes for a rewarding and nostalgic look at those days of the 1950s and 1960s.

HARTLEPOOL, *Town Wall Road c1955* H32036

MIDDLESBROUGH FROM THE AIR

MIDDLESBROUGH *from the air 1932* AF38954

FRANCIS FRITH'S CLEVELAND LIVING MEMORIES

THE MIDDLESBROUGH AND REDCAR AREA

MIDDLESBROUGH
The Transporter Bridge c1965 M71055

The Transporter Bridge was opened on 17 October 1911 by Prince Arthur of Connaught, whose father had opened Albert Park in 1868. It solved the problem of constructing a bridge over a busy shipping river where large vessels were trading or being built. Many such bridges were built in Europe at that time, but few now survive, and fewer still are in service. This bridge is now a symbol for the Middlesbrough municipality, and remains in operation.

THE MIDDLESBROUGH AND REDCAR AREA

MIDDLESBROUGH
The Town Hall and the Gardens c1965 M71091

The imposing Town Hall and Municipal Buildings were opened on 23 January 1889 by Edward, Prince of Wales and his wife Princess Alexandra. The architect was G G Hoskins. The gardens in the foreground were originally a cattle market in the 1880s, and subsequently a cycle track, skating rink and circus venue. The area was converted into ornamental gardens with a bandstand in 1901, and called Victoria Square.

MIDDLESBROUGH, *Albert Road c1965* M71060

The property on the left is of particular interest, because in about 1970 a large section of the older central Middlesbrough buildings was flattened to create the first major shopping mall - the Cleveland Centre. The loss of all these small shops and the Corporation Hotel was traumatic at the time, but many residents can no longer now remember them!

MIDDLESBROUGH
*Linthorpe Road
c1960* M71062

It is remarkable how little traffic we see here in contrast with present times. This section of Linthorpe Road has changed mainly in the shop owners. Very few remain the same, although Halfords (right) only moved in recent times. On the left stands the Wesleyan chapel, with the old ABC cinema further away on the right. The tower of St George's Congregational Church can be seen in the centre distance – it was demolished many years ago.

MIDDLESBROUGH
*The Park Entrance
c1965* M71045

Albert Park was given to the town in 1868 by the famous ironmaster Henry Bolckow, who spent some £30,000 in purchasing the land and preparing it. Prince Arthur, Duke of Connaught, in opening it, named it after his father, the Prince Consort, who had died in 1861. The cenotaph to commemorate those locally who died in the First World War was unveiled on 11 November 1922. Bronze plaques on the adjacent walls carry more than 3000 names.

THE MIDDLESBROUGH AND REDCAR AREA

▲ **MIDDLESBROUGH,** *Albert Park c1955* M71021

Just inside the ornamental gates we can see the original house of the Park Curator, which today serves as a small café. The Dorman Museum, opened in 1904, lies just beyond the gates. The statue on the left is of Henry Bolckow, which was placed there in 1925; more recently it was re-sited in central Middlesbrough. The clock on its tall pillar was presented to the town in 1900.

◄ **MIDDLESBROUGH**
*Albert Park,
the Fountain c1955*
M71007

This ornamental fountain was provided in 1896 by Joseph Pease, one of the Owners of the Middlesbrough Estate, and it was traditionally surrounded by beautiful flower beds. Restoration work is currently being undertaken on these features. The refreshment rooms on the right no longer survive, but were presented to the town in 1874 by Henry Bolckow, who died in 1878.

FRANCIS FRITH'S CLEVELAND LIVING MEMORIES

▲ **MIDDLESBROUGH,**
The Lake, Albert Park c1955 M71016

How fortunate that the industrial town of Middlesbrough could boast such a tranquil feature in its midst! The boating lake was an original feature from 1868, and was placed at the east end of the main avenue through the park. In recent times it has been beautifully restored, and now attracts many water birds.

▶ *detail from* M71016

THE MIDDLESBROUGH AND REDCAR AREA

MIDDLESBROUGH
Pallister Park c1955
M71030

Land for an ornamental park and recreation ground, an area of some 30 acres in North Ormesby, was given to the town by Councillor and Mrs J G Pallister. It was opened in 1929, and included hard tennis courts, bowling greens and a putting green. The Queen opened a major restoration of the park's facilities in 1993.

MARTON IN CLEVELAND, *The Church c1960* M132013

This ancient church - originally Norman - is dedicated to St Cuthbert. Buried in its churchyard are the two ironmaster founders of Middlesbrough's original wealth - Henry Bolckow and his business partner John Vaughan. On display inside the church is the baptism register recording that the world-famous navigator and explorer Captain James Cook was christened here on 3 November 1728.

FRANCIS FRITH'S CLEVELAND LIVING MEMORIES

▶ **MARTON IN CLEVELAND**
The Captain Cook Memorial School c1955
M132014

Built in stone from the original Marton Hall in 1850 to serve the village of Marton, this Victorian building operated as the local school until 1963, when a modern building replaced it nearby. It has since been used as a children's nursery, and stands at the junction of Stokesley Road and The Grove.

◀ **MARTON IN CLEVELAND**
The Grove c1960
M132007

There cannot be a leafier lane than this within the boundaries of Middlesbrough. Lying just outside the eastern edge of Stewart Park, The Grove represents one of the most exclusive local neighbourhoods, but more houses have been built since this view was taken, and traffic restrictions have been applied.

THE MIDDLESBROUGH AND REDCAR AREA

▲ **MARTON IN CLEVELAND,** *The Park c1965* M132026

Stewart Park was originally the grounds of Marton Hall, the magnificent residence of Henry Bolckow which he built in the 1850s, and filled with valuable works of art. As the Bolckows died out, Councillor Thomas Dormand Stewart paid £25,000 for the house and grounds in 1923 and presented them to the town. Marton Hall was demolished in 1960. The very large conservatory we see here was built in 1963 and demolished in 1997. The Captain Cook Birthplace Museum was built here in 1978, and is well worth a visit.

◄ **MARTON IN CLEVELAND**
The Shopping Centre c1965 M132053

A typical post Second World War shopping centre, with a range of shops designed to meet most of the local needs of those living in these suburbs of Middlesbrough. A Mobil petrol filling station (now closed) can be seen in the distance, serving these typical cars of the period. Many more housing estates have now been built in Marton, and the car park is much busier today.

FRANCIS FRITH'S CLEVELAND LIVING MEMORIES

▶ **MARTON IN CLEVELAND**
Stokesley Road c1965
M132033

This road runs south to Stokesley, some five miles away. The Mobil petrol station is just off to the left - they were evidently offering Green Shield Stamps in return for purchases at that time. The traffic here today is phenomenal, and lights now control the crossroads in the middle distance. The fields in the background are now filled with houses.

THE MIDDLESBROUGH AND REDCAR AREA

◄ **MARTON IN CLEVELAND**
Stokesley Road c1965
M132041

We are looking north towards Stewart Park and Middlesbrough beyond. The old church and churchyard lie in the trees on the left, and the old wooden church hall - now gone - can be seen in the right foreground. On the left is the end of a long and attractive terrace of Victorian brick houses, which still survives.

detail of M132041

▼ **ORMESBY,** *The Parish Church c1955* O45003

Ormesby is an ancient community with Saxon and Viking origins. St Cuthbert's Parish Church represents a mixture of periods and styles, the tower and spire being only about one hundred years old. 'Ormesby' means 'the settlement owned by Orm', which confirms that this area has been inhabited continuously for at least one thousand years.

▶ **ORMESBY**
The Church Hall and the Roundabout c1965 O45018

A major roundabout lies just off to the right, at the junction of Ormesby High Street and Cargo Fleet Lane, and this view looks north towards Middlesbrough. Ormesby still boasts some attractive buildings, and these include the church hall on the right and the Victorian villas in the centre.

THE MIDDLESBROUGH AND REDCAR AREA

◀ **ORMESBY**
The High Street c1965 O45043

This is a very interesting view, because the old Red Lion Inn in the centre must have been demolished very soon after this photograph was taken. It was sacrificed in a road-widening scheme, and replaced by the Fountain public house, which was set back in line with the ancient row of almshouses we see here on the left.

▶ **ORMESBY,** *The High Street c1965* O45020

Compare this view with No O45043, and note the cottage on the right with the broad light-coloured band above the front door running across the house front. This building appears in both pictures. We can see the signboard for the new Fountain public house on the left beside the street lamp, but the pub is set back out of sight. The major roundabout is visible at the end of the road.

▶ **ORMESBY**
*Ormesby Bank
c1965* 045037

This famous and quite steep incline leads southwards to Nunthorpe and Guisborough. It now carries considerably more traffic, and speeds are closely monitored by the police; it is dominated by large estates built in the fields visible on the left. The motor cycle with sidecar (centre) is now a rare sight.

THE MIDDLESBROUGH AND REDCAR AREA

◀ **ORMESBY**
The Market c1965
O45011

Here we see a small modern shopping centre with a necessary car park, containing some interesting models of yesteryear - for instance Ford Anglia and Ford Cortina, Austin, Rover, Vauxhall Velox and Triumph Herald. The prominent sign includes a clock, calendar and temperature gauge, and it can also be seen in O45020 (page 27).

THE MIDDLESBROUGH AND REDCAR AREA

ORMESBY
Lealholm Crescent
c1965 045007

This view is taken on Ormesby Road, looking south towards the junction with Ladgate Lane in the distance. Beyond are the grounds of the National Trust property Ormesby Hall, formerly the ancestral home of the Pennyman family. Lealholm Crescent is the service road in front of the parade of shops.

FRANCIS FRITH'S CLEVELAND LIVING MEMORIES

▶ **ORMESBY**
Lealholm Crescent c1965 O45008

Here we have a closer view, looking north, of the shopping parade soon after its construction. The forecourt of a National petrol station can be seen beyond the main building. The local shops include Appletons the baker's, a small supermarket, a chemist's and an off-licence.

◀ **TEESVILLE**
Eston Grammar School c1965 T121001

The Grammar School, on Normanby Road, South Bank was opened in 1955. It was described as 'long desired', and was provided by the North Riding County Council in conjunction with Eston Urban District Council. Changes in administrative boundaries and education policy were later to alter its status significantly. The buildings are now part of the Gillbrook Technology College.

THE MIDDLESBROUGH AND REDCAR AREA

▲ **GRANGETOWN,** *The Recreation Ground, the Gardens c1965* T121004

We are looking east towards some of the cooling towers of the huge Imperial Chemical Industries Wilton Site. These gardens offer a tranquil setting amidst the nearby heavy industries of steel and chemicals. They are close to the busy trunk road between Middlesbrough and Redcar.

◄ **GRANGETOWN**
The Bowling Green c1965 G88006

Lying close to the gardens in picture T121004, the bowling green is another representation of rest and recreation in an area surrounded by heavy industry. The photographer has managed to avoid the industrial backdrop on this occasion. Sad to say, this area is not as well maintained at the present time.

FRANCIS FRITH'S CLEVELAND LIVING MEMORIES

▶ **GRANGETOWN**
The Tennis Courts c1965
G88009

The bowling pavilion on the right, and some of the local housing is in the background. We are reminded of the importance which local authorities placed upon the provision of recreational facilities after the Second World War.

THE MIDDLESBROUGH AND REDCAR AREA

◀ **GRANGETOWN**
*The Paddling Pool
c1965* G88013

A rather less likely facility in the same park area is the children's playground, which includes an attractive paddling pool. Water has always had a fascination for the young. Industrial chimneys can be seen in the background on the left.

FAR LEFT:
detail of G88013

FRANCIS FRITH'S CLEVELAND LIVING MEMORIES

▶ **GRANGETOWN**
The Golf Course and the Cleveland Hills c1960 G88044

This peaceful scene was taken just off the Middlesbrough to Redcar trunk road, with the buildings of the former Stapylton School in the background on the right. The Cleveland Hills in the background represent the northern edge of the North Yorkshire Moors area.

◀ **GRANGETOWN**
The Broadway c1955 G88015

How amazing to see such a lack of road traffic by comparison with today! The Broadway is in practice a section of the main trunk road between Middlesbrough and Redcar. Grangetown developed around the old Grange Farm, when a local iron works was established here by Bolckow and Vaughan in the early 1850s.

THE MIDDLESBROUGH AND REDCAR AREA

▲ **GRANGETOWN,** *Birchington Avenue c1955* G88002

This major avenue crosses the Broadway at Grangetown, and illustrates the high quality housing originally provided for the local steel industry. Also evident are the overhead wires of the trolley bus system which served this part of Teesside from 1919 to 1971, provided by the Teesside Railless Traction Company.

◀ **GRANGETOWN**
Bolckow Road c1960
G88019

Bolckow Road was the busy commercial centre of the Grangetown community, as we can see here from the wide selection of local shops and the parish church of St Matthew in the centre. The road off to the left in the foreground is Birchington Avenue. Sad to say, the scene here today is one of decline in this community.

FRANCIS FRITH'S CLEVELAND LIVING MEMORIES

▶ **WILTON**
The ICI Plant at Night
c1965 W200001

This spectacular view was taken southwards towards the Eston Hills, and shows the great ICI Wilton Works, which was developed after the Second World War - the site extended for almost two miles. At its peak more than 15,000 people worked here, and the significant employment which it offered was very important to the local economy. It is still a large site, but is now operated by a variety of international chemical companies.

THE MIDDLESBROUGH AND REDCAR AREA

◀ **REDCAR**
Coatham Enclosure, the Boating Lake c1955 R16013

The Coatham Enclosure was created from an area of sand dunes, and a retaining wall - the New Promenade - was built to protect the area from the blowing sand. This boating lake opened in 1930. The indoor public baths in the centre background were opened in 1900, but they were eventually demolished in 1978, to be re-instated within a new building on the same site.

FAR LEFT:
detail of R16013

FRANCIS FRITH'S CLEVELAND LIVING MEMORIES

THE MIDDLESBROUGH AND REDCAR AREA

REDCAR
The Town Clock c1955
R16001

This is a famous town centre view. This clock was originally a project by the Redcar Urban District Council to celebrate the coronation of King Edward VII in 1902. It was later postponed, and eventually completed in 1912 as a memorial to the King, who had died in 1911. In more recent years its maintenance has become a problem, and it has not worked for some considerable time.

FRANCIS FRITH'S CLEVELAND LIVING MEMORIES

▶ **REDCAR**
The High Street c1960 R16048

Plenty of nostalgia here! A single-decker United bus allows passengers to disembark, having travelled all the way from Osmotherley. The Hinton's grocery shop on the right appears to be an early form of supermarket. The National Provincial Bank building stands on the left. The clock tower lies just off to the right.

◀ **REDCAR**
The High Street c1960
R16047

This was taken with only a few minutes difference from No R16048 - some of the people are standing in the same positions! We get a better view of the elegant bank building on the left. The double-decker United bus is a No 63 from Middlesbrough. Well-known shops here include Burtons, Woolworths and Timpsons.

▲ **REDCAR,** *The High Street c1965* R16078

We are looking back the other way from R16047, with Sparks bakery and restaurant next door to the local branch of W H Smith (left). High on the wall in the centre is the sign for the Redcar Literary Institute – the annual subscription was 10s. Clothing styles have changed - no anoraks and trainers here!

◄ **REDCAR**
The High Street c1960
R16045

This photograph shows an interesting row of cars and motorcycles of the period - few will have survived the intervening years. The Middlesbrough Co-operative store is on the right. Many of these properties were originally private houses, looking out across what became one of the widest high streets in the area. There is not a moving vehicle in sight!

THE MIDDLESBROUGH AND REDCAR AREA

REDCAR
The High Street c1955
R16005

This is another section of the main shopping centre, with the Red Lion Hotel on the left, Goodswens the butcher's in the centre, close to the grocer's shop of Pybus Brothers, and Hancocks on the corner - 'hatters, glovers and hosiers'. The traffic level is remarkably low, and it is safe to ride a bicycle.

FRANCIS FRITH'S CLEVELAND LIVING MEMORIES

▼ **REDCAR**, *The Beach c1955* R16041

Redcar's popularity for the past 150 years has largely depended upon the attractions of the sea and the beach. A group of roundabouts and swings offers entertainment for the children. Notice how few of the people shown are in swimming costumes - perhaps there was a chill wind blowing off the sea?

▶ **REDCAR**
The Promenade c1960
R16042

Here we have a busy Promenade view with plenty of warm clothing in evidence. Cafés across the road include Kings, the Belmont, and in the distance, Pybus Brothers, near to the Palace Cinema. The cinema also offered café facilities, but closed as a cinema within a year or two of this picture being taken.

THE MIDDLESBROUGH AND REDCAR AREA

◀ **REDCAR**
The Beach c1955
R16052

Few people can now remember how crowded the beach became on a warm summer day - the scenes here were comparable with Blackpool Beach. Holidaymakers came to stay in Redcar after the Second World War, before cheap foreign holidays were developed; many of them came from Scotland and the West Riding. It would be difficult to find a space for your deckchair!

▶ **REDCAR**
The Bowling Green c1960 R16057

A ladies' bowls match is in progress in the peaceful setting of Zetland Park, at the start of the Coast Road to Marske. Lord Zetland had given the town six acres of land, which was developed and opened in 1924; it originally also included tennis courts and gardens, a lake and an aviary.

FRANCIS FRITH'S CLEVELAND LIVING MEMORIES

SALTBURN BY THE SEA *from the air 1932* AF38948

SALTBURN AND EAST CLEVELAND

MARSKE BY THE SEA
Cliff House c1955 M40014

Cliff House was built in the mid 19th century by the Pease family, who owned the nearby Upleatham Ironstone Mines. It was sold to the Holiday Fellowship organisation before the Second World War. In later years it became semi-derelict before being bought by the Church Army for a retirement home.

SALTBURN AND EAST CLEVELAND

MARSKE BY THE SEA
Marske Hall c1960 M40031

One of the outstanding buildings in the area, Marske Hall was built in 1625 for Sir William Pennyman, whose descendants later settled at Ormesby Hall. Subsequently the Lowthers and then the Dundas family lived here, the latter eventually taking the Zetland title. Briefly a private school after the Second World War, the Hall was then given by Lord Zetland to the Leonard Cheshire Foundation in 1961.

MARSKE BY THE SEA, *The High Street c1960* M40039

This view shows Marske High Street on a quiet day, with two vehicles from the United Bus Company on their routes between Redcar and Saltburn. Compared with an identical view from 1917, the main difference is the later introduction of the tall poles carrying electricity and telephone wires and also street lamps.

FRANCIS FRITH'S CLEVELAND LIVING MEMORIES

▼ **MARSKE BY THE SEA,** *The High Street c1960* M40038

Rather curiously, the High Street turns sharp right at this road junction, and heads down to the beach. The road in the centre distance is the Coast Road to Redcar. The Ship Inn on the right was re-built in the Tudor style in 1932, using oak beams from two famous wooden battleships for its external decoration.

▶ **MARSKE BY THE SEA**
The Valley Gardens and the High Street c1955 M40015

This is the seaward end of the High Street, which runs down onto the beach. In an earlier period this area included beautiful sheltered gardens and a bandstand. Allotments were also established in the First World War to ease potential food shortages. A boat on a trailer here (left) confirms the ancient links between this community and the sea.

SALTBURN AND EAST CLEVELAND

◀ **MARSKE BY THE SEA**
The Beach, looking South c1955 M40021

The beaches between Marske and Saltburn were considered to be of the highest quality, with racing events and speed records for cars and motor cycles taking place from 1906 until after the Second World War. The tents in this view indicate that this is the 1950s period - it would be surprising to find them put up on the beach today. Huntcliffe beyond Saltburn falls steeply into the sea in the distance.

▶ **MARSKE BY THE SEA**
The Beach c1955 M40024

Fishing cobles on their wheeled trailers are drawn up above the high tide watermark, and two of the familiar old rusty tractors which pull the boats in and out of the sea can be seen. The end of the High Street lies in the centre, and Cliff House stands just out of view on the right.

UPLEATHAM
The Church c1960
U16002

One of Cleveland's famous landmarks, the old church stands on the site of earlier Saxon and Norman churches. It was abandoned as a place of worship in 1836, and much of it was subsequently demolished, which led to the claim in later years that it was 'the smallest church in England'. It lies in an isolated site outside the village, and is dedicated to St Andrew.

SALTBURN BY THE SEA
Albion Terrace c1955
S51047

We are looking along Albion Terrace into Station Street, with the impressive portico of the station entrance on the left in the distance. The railway arrived in Saltburn in 1861. The imposing Queen Hotel in the centre was built in 1875. The Primitive Methodist church on this side of the hotel was completed in 1910; it became a community centre in the 1970s.

SALTBURN AND EAST CLEVELAND

▲ **SALTBURN BY THE SEA,** *Station Street c1955* S51069

We are looking in the opposite direction to S51047 towards Albion Terrace, with the Queen Hotel and the Primitive Methodist church just visible on the left-hand side of the street. Again on the left we can see a good example of the typical Saltburn glass and cast iron canopies to keep pedestrians sheltered. Also typical of Saltburn is the extensive mandatory use of white firebricks from the Pease Company for the construction of the town centre.

◀ **SALTBURN BY THE SEA**
The Zetland Hotel c1955
S51139

The Stockton and Darlington Railway Company built the Zetland Hotel as a flagship project, hoping to attract other developers to the town as the concept of a new spa resort was being pursued. It opened in 1863, and the railway brought guests to a special platform at the rear of the hotel. Within the last twenty years the building has been converted into individual private apartments.

SALTBURN BY THE SEA
Brockley Hall c1965
S51262

A number of quality villas were planned during the 1860s in the early development of Saltburn, although not all of them materialised. This elegant building, which stands not far from the Zetland Hotel, did get built, originally as a private residence, but in later years it became a holiday home for a Christian charitable organisation.

SALTBURN BY THE SEA, The Toll Bridge c1955 S51143
Built by the Wharton family of Skelton Castle for ease of access across Saltburn Glen, the toll bridge was completed in 1869. It stood 120ft high at the centre. It cost a halfpenny for pedestrians when it opened - hence it became known as 'The Ha'penny Bridge'. Its condition gradually deteriorated, and it was demolished by explosives in spectacular fashion in 1974.

SALTBURN AND EAST CLEVELAND

SALTBURN BY THE SEA
The Italian Garden, Valley Gardens c1955
S51097

This attractive feature was part of the Valley Gardens site in Saltburn Glen, and was originally established in the 1860s when the concept of an Italian garden was very fashionable. Some fifty years later it was illuminated by lanterns and candles in the evenings, and was described as 'one of the finest pieces of floral artistry in the Kingdom'. Some elements of it still remain.

SALTBURN BY THE SEA, *The Tea Gardens c1955* S51081

Here we see another restful feature in the Valley Gardens, but this is a later design. The area was originally a croquet lawn, established in 1864. The woodland environment made an attractive setting for occasional light entertainment - note the stage - and this arena would be a real sun trap owing to its sheltered position.

SALTBURN BY THE SEA
The Miniature Railway
c1955 S51058

Always a highly popular attraction, the miniature railway was opened in the Valley Gardens in 1947. It has since undergone various changes of ownership and modifications to the line and equipment, but its appeal to visitors young and old has never waned.

FRANCIS FRITH'S CLEVELAND LIVING MEMORIES

▼ **SALTBURN BY THE SEA,** *Hazelgrove Caravan Site c1955* S51186

The Hazelgrove Glen was given to Saltburn by the Marquis of Zetland in 1899; it became the town's first free park in 1904, after some initial reluctance by the Town Council to adopt and develop it. In the 1870s this area had been earmarked to be the first town cemetery, but that plan was never implemented. It has become a much more congested caravan site today.

▶ **SALTBURN BY THE SEA**
The Cliff Tramway and the Pier c1955 S51099

The cliff tramway was opened in 1884, replacing an earlier vertical hoist installed in 1870. Using water ballast to operate it, it still works today, making the journey between town and beach a much easier one. The pier opened in 1869, and was originally 1500ft long. Since that time various incidents as well as corrosion have considerably shortened it, but it remains much cherished and cared for today, thanks to its own Preservation Society.

SALTBURN AND EAST CLEVELAND

◀ SALTBURN BY THE SEA
Saltburn Bank and the Pier c1960 S51215

Road access between the seashore cottages of old Saltburn and the new town required a steep incline, which has been the scene of some spectacular runaway vehicle crashes. The Bank Café lies on the right, and it is clearly a warm summer day in view of the number of parked cars at the bottom of the hill.

▶ SALTBURN BY THE SEA
The Beach and Huntcliffe c1960 S51216

A fun fair can be seen in the foreground, and the beach entertains many visitors in this view of old Saltburn, with the Ship Inn just visible over the shoulder of Cat Nab (right). The Beach Café (centre) is doing good business, and the imposing outline of Huntcliffe dominates in the distance. The shore bridge on the left has been demolished by rough seas or river floods on a number of occasions.

SKELTON
Church Lane c1965
S285026

These old stone cottages lie on the approach to Skelton Castle, and the wide gateway to the left beyond them is the start of the driveway up to the castle. The tower of All Saints' Church, which stands within the castle grounds, can be seen above the trees; it was founded in 1325 and re-built in 1785. The last regular service in this church took place in 1906.

SKELTON
The Castle c1965
S285020

The original castle was built by the legendary Robert de Brus in 1140. Many other famous families have also been associated with this estate, including the Fauconbergs, the Conyers, the Trotters, the Hall Stevensons and the Whartons. Over the centuries many alterations were made to the castle fabric, but its present appearance dates back to the early 1800s

SALTBURN AND EAST CLEVELAND

▲ **SKELTON,** *The Castle Gardens c1965* S285024

This view shows part of the original castle moat, which was drained in 1862. At that time the rose garden was created, which lies within this beautiful woodland setting.

◄ **SKELTON**
West End c1955 S285011

Here we see the main road which passes through Skelton, with the war memorial sited in a triangular lawn to the right. The car is heading towards Whitby, and just beyond the tallest building on the left, which is now demolished, lies the Duke William public house.

FRANCIS FRITH'S CLEVELAND LIVING MEMORIES

▶ **SKELTON**
The Hills c1965 S285030

This is a quiet corner of Skelton on a narrow lane in the area called The Hills – we can clearly see the rural nature of the surrounding countryside. Looking at this view, it is hard to believe that many of the towns and villages of East Cleveland were industrially based, but indeed they were largely dependant on ironstone mining for almost a century between the 1850s and the 1950s. The earth mounds in the foreground may be relics of those activities, but the houses are modern.

SALTBURN AND EAST CLEVELAND

◀ **BROTTON**
The High Street c1955
B317003

Brotton is another settlement with an ancient history; it was also seriously influenced by the ironstone industry at a later date. Kilton Castle, seat of the de Thweng family, lies in the immediate neighbourhood. The population of Brotton grew from 330 in 1861 to 2672 in 1871 as a result of the discovery of local ironstone. This quiet scene shows the main Whitby to Guisborough road running past leafy gardens. The parish church is hidden near the car on the right-hand side of the road.

BROTTON
The High Street c1955
B317008

We are looking eastwards from the end of Brotton High Street, and the chimneys of the Skinningrove iron and steel works can be seen in the distance. At the far end of the left-hand row of houses we can just see the gable end of the Cottage Hospital, built in 1874 by Bell Brothers for the casualties inevitably arising from the local ironstone mining operations. The post office stands next to the letter box (left).

SKINNINGROVE, *The Jetty c1955* S286013
The jetty was constructed by the Skinningrove Iron Company in 1886 to enable the products from their works to be exported. A railway line ran directly from the works down an incline and along the jetty to make the transfer of material into the ships an easy operation. Fishing cobles owned by Skinningrove families are drawn up on the beach in the foreground.

SALTBURN AND EAST CLEVELAND

SKINNINGROVE
The Cliffs c1955
S286014

The isolated village of Skinningrove lies behind the camera – it is a community used to hardships and exposed to fierce winter weather. The high road over to Boulby can be seen on the right, passing the traditional pigeon lofts. The beck in the foreground still runs brown with the colour of the local ironstone seams.

LOFTUS, *Mill Bank c1960* L159028

The lane down to Skinningrove village runs off at the bottom left-hand corner. On the skyline we can just see the overhead tramway carrying buckets of ironstone from one of the mines. The newly widened road begins to rise in the distance up to Loftus, whilst the United Bus Company bus stops are placed in neat lay-bys. The former Loftus watermill buildings lie off to the right of this view.

LOFTUS
Westfield Terrace c1960
L159034a

The Congregational church on the right was opened in 1906, and stands on the corner of the High Street with Westfield Terrace. Across the High Street, the road runs up to Liverton Mines. Loftus has suffered from a fluctuating economy over the past 150 years, knowing perhaps more bad times than good, but remaining ever optimistic about its future.

LOFTUS
Westfield Terrace c1960
L159034b

Here we have a view of some quality terraced houses higher up the same street, with the Congregational church still visible (left). Bay windows, white firebricks and front gardens give the properties an original touch of class. We can see a window cleaner at work, with his ladder cart on the roadway.

SALTBURN AND EAST CLEVELAND

▲ **LOFTUS,** *Station Road c1960* L159033

The Station Hotel stands to the left, and the road up to Liverton Mines rises in the distance. The last rail passenger service through Loftus station was in May 1960, and the line had operated with steam engines until two years earlier; the large buildings in the distance were part of the station, and are now demolished.

◄ **LOFTUS**
High Town Lane c1960
L159040

This is a quaint corner of Loftus, which here looks totally unsuited for the traffic of the present day. A pedestrian footbridge known as Haugh Bridge on the left offers some protection on the sharp bend, and a strongly flowing stream runs under the road at this point. The tower of the parish church rises in the distance. This lane is called Dam Street at its junction with the High Street.

MOORSHOLM
The Plough Inn c1960 M323001

This imposing edifice, with a front porch of great style, is perhaps surprisingly grand for such a small village on the edge of the North Yorkshire Moors. The outside staircase would suggest that the living quarters were entirely separate from the downstairs business. This hostelry is today known as the Toad Hall Arms, and stands at the northern end of the High Street.

MOORSHOLM
The Church c1960 M323003

A substantial stone building of pleasing proportions, with a matching boundary wall, St Mary's Church was built in 1892 and stands on the High Street. The ladder suggests that some kind of roof maintenance work was in progress when the photographer was passing.

SALTBURN AND EAST CLEVELAND

▲ **MOORSHOLM,** *The High Street c1960* M323006

This was definitely a traffic-free zone when the photographer called! The village shop (right) stands slightly higher than the terraced houses on either side, and all are built in local stone. Today the shop has reverted to being a private dwelling. 'Moorsholm Docks' can also be found on the High Street - in reality, a set of stone drinking troughs for passing animals.

◀ **GUISBOROUGH**
The Fox Inn, Bow Street c1960 G66049

The Fox Inn dominates this view up Bow Street to the tall Market Cross, which we can just see at the head of Westgate in the distance. The newsagents and tobacconists shop – Robinsons, centre - displays the wealth of bold advertising material so typical of the period. This was the main road from Whitby to Teesside - how quiet it was on this occasion!

SALTBURN AND EAST CLEVELAND

GUISBOROUGH
Westgate c1955
G66016

What a difference a few well-groomed trees make to this street scene. We can just see the Market Cross on the right in the distance. Two vehicles from the United Bus Company pick up passengers, the nearer one (centre right) serving the Great Ayton to Redcar route. Behind it, the tall stone building was the Midland Bank.

GUISBOROUGH
The Market Cross and Westgate c1955
G66002

This photograph shows the wide expanse of Westgate, a street typical of the old market towns in the area: there was room for animals being driven to market, market stalls, and all the people who came into town from the surrounding districts on market days. The old Town Hall can just be seen in the left foreground, and the view looks towards Middlesbrough.

GUISBOROUGH
Westgate c1955 G66024

Here we have a clearer view of the tall Town Hall building to the right, and beyond it lies the premises of the National Provincial Bank. The tower of the parish church of St Nicholas can just be seen in the distance. At this date Church Street, leading out of the Market Place, was very narrow. It was widened in 1962. Cafés have always been a prominent feature in the town – there are at least three on the left.

SALTBURN AND EAST CLEVELAND

▲ **GUISBOROUGH,** *Westgate c1955* G66028

The cobbled areas to the sides of the road remain an attractive feature today, although they are usually covered in motor cars. Behind one of the nearer trees on the left stands the tall Methodist chapel, built in 1907 originally as a Primitive Methodist place of worship. Close by to the left of the chapel stands the Kings Head Inn - an interesting neighbour!

◄ **GUISBOROUGH**
The Grammar School c1955 G66012

The Grammar School was an ancient foundation: its original founder and benefactor was Prior Pursglove in 1561, in the reign of Elizabeth I. The school was elegantly re-built in 1887, and these buildings are hidden behind the parish church. It lost its grammar school status in 1973, when comprehensive education principles were being introduced nationally.

GUISBOROUGH
The Applegarth c1955
G66011

This photograph is a peaceful distant view of the remains of the ancient Guisborough Priory, which flourished, but with various setbacks, in the period 1120-1538. It became a very wealthy foundation before the Dissolution of the Monasteries undertaken by Henry VIII in the late 1530s. The east end of the main priory building is shown here, neatly framing the tower of the parish church. Guisborough was regarded for many centuries as the capital of ancient Cleveland.

HUTTON
The Village c1955 H489020

This secluded community lies in a wooded valley on the outskirts of Guisborough. Some of the people who lived here were employed in the neighbouring ironstone mines, and others at nearby Hutton Hall, built in the 1860s for Sir Joseph Whitwell Pease. Hutton was known as the 'Model Village' or the 'Alpine Village' one hundred years ago.

detail of G66011

SALTBURN AND EAST CLEVELAND

FRANCIS FRITH'S CLEVELAND LIVING MEMORIES

STOCKTON ON TEES FROM THE AIR

STOCKTON ON TEES *from the air 1955* AFR25525

THE STOCKTON AREA

LEVEN BRIDGE
The Bridge and the Falls c1955 L507002

The River Leven flows through Stokesley, Hutton Rudby and Crathorne before passing under Leven Bridge and joining the River Tees at Yarm. The road bridge shown here is narrow, but it carries heavy traffic volumes between Yarm and the southern edge of Middlesbrough. The distant hillside is dotted with many henhouses serving about 4,000 free range chickens.

THE STOCKTON AREA

LEVEN BRIDGE
The Village c1955
L507005

A popular stop-off for cyclists and walkers from the local towns long ago, this small settlement included the well known Cross Keys Inn, now derelict - as are most of the other buildings we see here. When the river is in flood, it also flows through the arches on the extreme right. A family stand by the high weir in the foreground. This is the site of an ancient watermill.

YARM, *The Friarage c1955* Y17001
One of the important historic buildings of Yarm, this mansion was built in 1770 on the site of the ancient Friary, using some of the stones from the original building. In the late 1970s it was purchased from an industrial corporation to become the focus of the new Yarm School, now a flourishing independent educational establishment.

FRANCIS FRITH'S CLEVELAND LIVING MEMORIES

▶ **YARM**
*The High Street
c1960* Y17020

We are looking north towards Yarm Bridge, with Stockton beyond. The Green Tree Inn on the right is a reminder of the remarkable number of public houses in Yarm; several of these were busy coaching inns with stabling to the rear for horses in the era of the stagecoaches between 1700 and 1840.

THE STOCKTON AREA

◀ **YARM**
The High Street c1955
Y17003

Yarm has a remarkably wide High Street, typical of many North Riding market towns. The large areas of cobblestones now allow parking for the vast numbers of cars to be found visiting or based in Yarm. The three-storey elegant town house buildings help to make Yarm a very attractive place in which to live.

▲ **YARM,** *The High Street 1963* Y17012

We are looking south, with a good view of Yarm Town Hall, built in 1710 and standing in splendid isolation in the centre of the High Street. The high chimney visible over the roof tops served a traditional skinyard treating sheep skins and other animal skins. The town sits in a big loop of the River Tees, and has on rare occasions in the past seen several feet of floodwater standing in the High Street.

YARM
*The High Street
c1965* Y17013

Just behind the camera at the north end of the town lies Yarm Bridge, reminding us that for centuries the River Tees was navigable; Yarm operated as an important port, until it was superseded later by Stockton and Middlesbrough. The market held in the High Street was widely famous, particularly for horse trading and for the selling of dairy products, especially cheeses.

THE STOCKTON AREA

FRANCIS FRITH'S CLEVELAND LIVING MEMORIES

▶ TEESSIDE AIRPORT
c1965 T120301

Originally built as a Second World War base for heavy bombers flying to Europe, the airport has gradually developed into a busy centre for UK domestic routes, holiday flights and scheduled flights into some major European cities and further afield. It has one of the longest runways in the country, and has been known as Teesside International Airport for some years.

◀ THORNABY ON TEES
The Five Lamps 1957
T122001

This is a wonderful memory of a fascinating part of Teesside which was completely obliterated from the map not long after this photograph was taken. The Five Lamps area was full of character - small shops, old buildings, interesting people. The development of complex new road systems for Teesside removed everything you can see here. This is a picture full of human interest.

THE STOCKTON AREA

▲ **THORNABY ON TEES,** *Mandale Road and the Five Lamps 1957* T122002

This photograph was taken on the same occasion as T122001. Trams used to run along Mandale Road between Norton and North Ormesby, but that was more than seventy years ago. Thornaby Town Hall in the centre distance still survives - an elegant building constructed in 1890. At an earlier date Thornaby was known as South Stockton, and was part of the North Riding of Yorkshire.

◀ **THORNABY ON TEES**
The Victoria Bridge c1955
T122007

This elegant and also vital feature provides an important crossing of the River Tees. Earlier bridges across the river had existed at this point, but the Victoria Bridge opened in 1887, in the Queen's Golden Jubilee year, replacing one built in 1769. The river is clearly tidal here - the nearby Tees Barrage was not completed until late 1994, and it was formally opened by the Duke of Edinburgh in the summer of 1995.

FRANCIS FRITH'S CLEVELAND LIVING MEMORIES

▼ **STOCKTON ON TEES,** *The Town Hall c1955* S195024

The Town Hall stands prominently in the centre of the High Street and dates from 1735. Motor traffic levels were low when this photograph was taken - in later years severe restrictions and road re-design have been applied. The offices of the former National Provincial Bank - now NatWest - stand imposingly on the right.

▶ **STOCKTON ON TEES**
The High Street c1965
S195055

This view was taken from the Town Hall, with the Market Cross in the foreground, a 33ft-high column dating from 1768. Beyond in the centre of the road is the original Shambles building, an enclosed market erected in 1825. It is claimed that Stockton has the widest High Street in England - a good example of early town planning! The wonderful historic façade of the shops on the left was unforgivably removed in 1970 for a new shopping development.

THE STOCKTON AREA

◀ STOCKTON ON TEES
Dovecot Street c1965
S195050

We are looking westwards from the High Street into Dovecot Street. A major change was the demolition of the old Stockton Literary and Philosophical Institute - the tallest building to the right - not long after this picture was taken. On the left up the street we can just see the end gable of the Brunswick Methodist chapel - a very thriving church in the earlier history of the town; it still survives, but as a carpet warehouse.

▶ STOCKTON ON TEES
The High Street c1965 S195056

Cars parked down the centre of the High Street occupy the site of the historic outdoor town market, which still operates today and makes this area a very busy place on Wednesdays and Saturdays. Dovecot Street runs off to the right just behind the nearest bus. Some of the shop names remain familiar - others have since disappeared.

FRANCIS FRITH'S CLEVELAND LIVING MEMORIES

THE STOCKTON AREA

STOCKTON ON TEES
The High Street and the Parish Church c1955 S195020

We are looking in the other direction, to the north end of the High Street. The parish church tower stands prominently on the right, with the war memorial with its white columns in front. The present church dates from 1712. The tallest building across the road was M Robinson's Coliseum Department Store, now Debenhams. Beyond it is the former Globe Theatre, and Maxwell's Corner Shop stands in the centre distance.

STOCKTON ON TEES
Ropner Park c1965
S195060

The park, situated along the Yarm Road, was the gift of Sir Robert Ropner, and was opened by the Duke and Duchess of York on 4 October 1893. The very attractive fountain is evidently the centrepiece of an ornamental and floral display on this occasion, and a panel of flowers in the background marks a centenary in which the large cross on the bank no doubt has some significance.

NORTON ON TEES
The Parish Church c1955
N69006

Covered in ivy, the imposing and ancient structure of Norton parish church stands above the Green in a peaceful churchyard. Dedicated to St Mary the Virgin, the building has Saxon origins. Many of the eminent former residents of Stockton and Norton are buried here, and Thomas Sheraton, the world-famous furniture designer, was married in the church in 1779 – he was born in Stockton in 1751.

THE STOCKTON AREA

▲ **NORTON ON TEES,** *The Green c1955* N69008

Still a very pleasant open area near the church, the Green was once much bigger. One of the 18th-century vicars incorporated a large section of it into the grounds of the new vicarage with the Bishop's permission, enraging the local inhabitants. On the right is the old National School, built in 1838, but later used as a church hall and then as a community centre.

◄ **NORTON ON TEES**
The High Street c1965
N69016

Some of the local shops look out onto the large pond at the top end of Norton High Street, with the Unicorn public house on the corner just to the right of centre. The famous Duck Pond was originally constructed some centuries ago; it was lined with clay so that it retained its water even though it was located at one of the higher points in Norton.

NORTON ON TEES
The Green and the Duck Pond c1965
N69044

The photographer has taken his picture across the duck pond in order to get this interesting set of reflections. The properties we see here sit on the edge of Norton Green, with the High Street off to the right, and the church and vicarage a short distance up to the left. The pond looks well kept and clean at this time.

NORTON ON TEES, *Georgian Houses, the High Street c1965* N69021

Norton High Street is one of the surprise features in Teesside, with several elegant period houses nestling behind the trees which line the road verges. This was where some of the wealthy businessmen built their homes, when the village was separated from Stockton by green fields. Thank goodness, it is still a very pleasing environment to visit and explore.

THE STOCKTON AREA

NORTON ON TEES
The High Street c1955
N69011

Looking into the lower end of the High Street, this photograph illustrates the wide variety of small shops which continues to serve the Norton community. Some famous names, now gone, can be seen, including Sparks bakery and Newmans delicatessen. Were the shops more interesting then, or is it just nostalgia?

NORTON ON TEES, *The High Street c1955* N69012
This photograph was taken at almost the same point as N69011. The High Street leads towards Stockton in the centre. The property on the left is little changed today. The tall cross in the foreground has attractive Celtic carving and lettering, and was erected in 1897 by the inhabitants of Norton to mark the Diamond Jubilee of Queen Victoria. It is unusual, therefore, that it is not a memorial cross.

FRANCIS FRITH'S CLEVELAND LIVING MEMORIES

▼ **BILLINGHAM,** *The ICI Office Building c1960* B315012

This impressive building, constructed in 1958, was the headquarters of ICI's Agricultural Division until the early 1990s, serving a major international fertiliser business. It won a number of architectural awards. This must be an early photograph, because cars had later to be parked behind the building in the famous 'toast rack' construction on the right of this view, which is not yet built. Sad to say, the building is now unoccupied and semi-derelict.

▶ **BILLINGHAM**
The ICI Office Building c1965 B315056

This is a later photograph, with the futuristic-looking covered car park visible on the right - a car can just be seen there, giving an idea of its scale. Several hundred headquarters staff worked in this building, with the Division Board members' offices being on the seventh floor. The front entrance to the building has already been re-designed!

96

◀ BILLINGHAM
The Bowling Green
c1965 B315033

Here we have a clear, open view across the John Whitehead Park to the Stockton and Billingham Technical College in the distance, with the community centre just visible on the extreme left. The park was opened in 1953. The Billingham town shopping centre lies immediately behind the photographer. Recently the college operations have been moved to a new site by the River Tees, and these extensive buildings have been demolished.

▶ BILLINGHAM
The Shopping Centre
c1967 B315046

Billingham Town Centre was developed in the 1950s and 1960s, paid for largely by the local rates from the massive ICI factory in the neighbourhood, which employed almost 20,000 people at that time. The town centre design was quite visionary, and attracted several of the big retailers. As the years have passed, it has suffered from the loss of high employment in the area, and little re-development.

BILLINGHAM, *The Family Group Statue c1970* B315074

The founders of the modern Billingham Town Centre felt the need to introduce features which helped to take away the starkness of the new surroundings. This modern sculpture, in front of the art gallery, is very realistic in style, and serves to remind the passer-by of the importance of the family group within the structure of our present-day society. The Queen unveiled this statue in December 1967.

THE STOCKTON AREA

BILLINGHAM
The Town Centre
c1970 B315072

This view was taken further down the shopping precinct. In the distance are high-rise flats. Towards the right we can see part of the Billingham Forum Theatre, and nearer is the round glass-enclosed staircase to the art gallery. Trees and shrubs are used to break up the hard lines of the modern architecture. The weather canopies and the water feature have since been removed.

WOLVISTON, *Wynyard Road c1955* W201006

An ancient village, Wolviston lies close to Wynyard Hall, historically the family home of the Londonderry dynasty, whose fortune came from the ownership of several collieries and a port in County Durham. The present Wynyard Hall was completed in 1848, and many royal visitors were entertained there over the following hundred years. The war memorial commemorates the Wolviston casualties in both World Wars.

HARTLEPOOL FROM THE AIR

HARTLEPOOL *from the air 1972* AFA240107

THE HARTLEPOOL AREA

GREATHAM, *Sappers Corner c1955* G89003

The ancient settlement of Greatham lies halfway between Wolviston and Hartlepool. The large building on the right, at the entrance to the village, has always been known as Sappers Corner. Tommy Blumer built it for his fleet of buses, which was later taken over by the United Bus Company. He had been a sapper in the army in the First World War - hence the name. At this date it appears to be a petrol filling station, but it has had several other uses.

THE HARTLEPOOL AREA

GREATHAM
The High Street c1955
G89004

The Smiths Arms on the right is an attractive listed building. The second building from the left, with the lancet-style windows, is the Gray Memorial Hall - a Wesleyan school dating from 1903. The tall gabled building just beyond it is the Greatham Independent Methodist church, constructed in 1883.

GREATHAM, *The High Street c1955* G89011

As well as the Smiths Arms again visible in the centre distance, we can also see two more public houses here - the Hope and Anchor, the long white building on the right, and the Bull and Dog immediately beyond it! Note the Cerebos sign on the pub wall - the salt factory lay just outside the village; salt making was an ancient industry round here. Salt production ceased in 1970, but other products kept the factory going until the last year or so, when it was finally closed.

FRANCIS FRITH'S CLEVELAND LIVING MEMORIES

▼ **GREATHAM,** *The Grove c1955* G89009

An example of immediately post-war council housing, this street is now leafy and well-established, and largely in private ownership. It has a large circular grassed area at the head of the cul-de-sac in the distance. These houses would originally provide accommodation for workers at the local Cerebos factory and at the nearby steel works, for example.

▶ **GREATHAM**
Front Street c1955
G89005

On the left are the boundary walls of the Hospital of God at Greatham, founded in 1273 – this was not a hospital in the modern sense, but accommodation for the elderly and the poor, the earliest present buildings dating from a re-construction in 1803. On the right is the former Greatham Church School, founded in 1834, re-built in 1878, and enlarged in 1928. It now serves as the community centre.

THE HARTLEPOOL AREA

◀ **GREATHAM**
The Green c1955
G89007

The quaint old building to the right of centre still serves as the village post office and shop today. It is quite small, but it is elaborately decorated on its front outer wall. The village green is now fenced and council-owned. The road is heading towards the old Cerebos salt factory on the outskirts of the village.

▶ **SEATON CAREW**
The Green c1955
S85022

Most of these properties remain private residences today. Seaton Hall (left) is now a residential nursing home. This is a very attractive open area with interesting houses on three sides of a square, looking out to sea, which is behind the camera. An old Ford Prefect and a motor scooter help to date the view.

▼ SEATON CAREW, The Promenade c1965 S85023

The Marine Hotel (left), built in 1900, dominates this open sea front expanse. In the distance some of the houses on the green are visible. Hartlepool lies in the far distance on the right. The beach tents give the picture a period feeling. A bandstand once stood on the open area in front of the Marine Hotel.

▶ SEATON CAREW
The Promenade c1955
S85003

This earlier picture appears to have an open space where the Silver Dollar was later built. The neat chalets on the sea front have long gone. Beach vendors stands are offering tea, crisps and toffee apples. In the centre, in line with the Marine Hotel, a hut carries the sign 'Lost Children' - always a possibility at the seaside!

THE HARTLEPOOL AREA

◀ **SEATON CAREW**
Front Street
c1965 S85047

This sea front view also includes the Marine Hotel, along with some interesting cars of the period. The Silver Dollar Snack Bar (left), now called the Talk of the Town, still offers bingo, but has added a bowling alley. The Esspresso Coffee Bar next door evidently included dancing amongst its attractions. Road works are in progress outside.

▶ **SEATON CAREW**
The Sands c1965
S85024

Large cargo ships standing off the mouth of the River Tees are still a familiar sight today. Historically, Seaton Carew was a combination of fishing village (mainly in the 19th century and earlier) and holiday resort (late 19th and 20th century). Pony rides on the beach must have been more exciting than the traditional donkey rides. The sands here were renowned for their high quality.

SEATON CAREW
The Bus Station c1955
S85002

Very much an architectural relic of a former age, including its clock tower, the bus station looks very similar today, except that the high-level balcony on the left has gone. Beyond the building to the right is the John Collins Pleasure Beach. The big dipper (right) was dismantled in the 1970s - a big wheel had suffered a similar fate at an earlier date. The Cleveland Hills lie on the horizon.

SEATON CAREW, *The Swimming Baths c1955* S85001

Children are having a jolly time in the old baths, which were situated on the sea front near the Staincliffe Hotel. The baths were donated in 1914 by Sir William Gray, the famous local shipbuilder who had also founded the South Durham Steel and Iron Company in 1898. It is notable that the baths operated with salt water. They were demolished not long after this picture was taken.

THE HARTLEPOOL AREA

WEST HARTLEPOOL
Catcote Road c1960
W66029

Here we see modern post-war housing development in what was known as West Hartlepool until the two Hartlepools merged to form the County Borough of Hartlepool in 1967. The Red Admiral public house (left) remains today. It has altered its frontage to some extent, but has retained its original butterfly title – thank goodness, it has not changed it to one of the current more trendy names.

HARTLEPOOL, *The Harbour c1960* H32038
A fine open view of the harbour, with cabin cruisers, yachts and small fishing boats at anchor. Various types of working cranes add interest to the skyline, evidence of important port activities. The Dock Master's Office stands on the left, with its clock tower. An impressive marina is now established nearby.

HARTLEPOOL
Advertising c1960 H32080v

The side wall of this corner shop in Hartlepool is being used for the once familiar bill boards advertising Hovis bread, Swan Vesta matches and (a more modern product) Danish Lurpak butter. I Rosen and Son operated a drapers shop, with plenty of samples displayed in the windows. Their address is shown as No 69 and 71, and the property was situated in Musgrave Street.

HARTLEPOOL
Park Road and the Gardens c1965 H32072

This pretty garden lies on the corner of Park Road and York Road. How sad that this quiet place is now occupied by Titan House, a massive office building several storeys high and currently empty. A Shell petrol station can be seen on the left. Two of the older properties here - Lloyds Bank and the building beyond it (centre right) - still stand. St George's United Reformed Church stands behind the photographer.

HARTLEPOOL
The Memorial Gardens c1965 H32066

This impressive memorial commemorates the local dead in two World Wars, and stands in Victory Square. The Grand Hotel behind it still dominates this area. It was built in 1899 for the London and North Eastern Railway Company. The open space behind the trees on the left was known as the Bull Field. In the 1970s it was re-developed for the Civic Centre, magistrates' courts and police headquarters.

THE HARTLEPOOL AREA

◀ **HARTLEPOOL**
Lynn Street c1955
H32002

This was always a very popular shopping street, full of interest, with a wide variety of goods to meet all needs. How sad, then, that almost all of these properties in Lynn Street have now gone, and there are no shops left. All the character of the place we see here is lost. Well-known stores visible in this view include Woolworths, Boots and Timpsons, and the road traffic is almost non-existent.

FRANCIS FRITH'S CLEVELAND LIVING MEMORIES

▶ **HARTLEPOOL**
The Church and the Gardens c1965
H32090

The ancient abbey church of St Hilda stands proudly in the Headland area. It dates from about AD1190, and has been restored on many occasions over the centuries, most recently in 1924 and 1932. An Anglo-Saxon cemetery was discovered in this area. The influential de Brus family had close involvement with this church in later centuries. The gardens shown here have changed, but have survived.

◀ **HARTLEPOOL**
Town Wall Road c1955
H32036

The gardens we see in photograph H32090 can be seen just beyond the cars on the left, with St Hilda's Church behind the houses on the left. The large building on the right is the Harbour of Refuge - a splendid name for a seaside public house! Children play on the beach below the sea wall.

THE HARTLEPOOL AREA

▲ **HARTLEPOOL,** *The War Memorial c1955* W66021

This impressive war memorial lies on the Headland, and was originally dedicated in 1921 to those local men killed in the Great War. It was recently further dedicated to those local people who have died in all wars since then, and re-furbished with new boundary walls and paving. The 19th-century town houses of Cliff Terrace provide the background, and the Heugh Lighthouse built in 1847 lies just off to the right.

◄ **HARTLEPOOL**
The Sea Front c1955
H32022

More tall town houses look out to sea over the sea wall. These are known locally as Albion Terrace. Decorative fairy lights have been temporarily erected on tall poles for some kind of event or celebration. The solid stone shelter on the left is now gone, and over the sea wall today it is possible to see shipping movements and the navigational structure shown in picture H32100 on page 114.

HARTLEPOOL
The Harbour Wall
c1960 H32100

The Pilot's Pier light sits on a long promontory extending from the sea wall, and cargo shipping and the associated tug boats pass by it on their way in and out of the port. In the background on the right are some of the buildings of local heavy industry. The Dock Master's Office building can just be seen in front of the bridge of the vessel leaving harbour.

HARTLEPOOL, *Marine Drive c1955* H32021

This attractive terrace of houses lies close to the sea on the north side of the Headland, which is beyond the buildings in the centre distance. The North Sands area is a very exposed position, and a rough sea can be quite intimidating when the high tide comes in. The sea defences seen here are designed to cut the power of the waves on such occasions.

INDEX

Billingham 96-97, 98, 99
Brotton 64-65, 66
Grangetown 33, 34-35, 36-37
Greatham 102, 103, 104-105
Guisborough 71, 72-73, 74-75, 76-77
Hartlepool 13, 109, 110-111, 112-113, 114
Hutton 76-77
Leven Bridge 80, 81
Loftus 67, 68-69
Marske by the Sea 11, 50, 51, 52-53
Marton in Cleveland 21, 22-23, 24-25
Middlesbrough 16, 17, 18-19, 20, 21
Moorsholm 70-71
Norton on Tees 92, 93, 94, 95

Ormesby 26-27, 28-29, 30-31, 32-33
Redcar 38-39, 40-41, 42-43, 44-45, 46-47
Saltburn by the Sea 54, 55, 56, 57, 58-59, 60-61
Seaton Carew 105, 106-107, 108
Skelton 62-63, 64-65
Skinningrove 66, 67
Stockton on Tees 88-89, 90-91, 92-93
Teesside Airport 86-87
Teesville 32
Thornaby on Tees 86, 87
Upleatham 54-55
Wilton 38-39
Wolviston 99
Yarm 81, 82-83, 84-85

FRITH PRODUCTS & SERVICES

Francis Frith would doubtless be pleased to know that the pioneering publishing venture he started in 1860 still continues today. Over a hundred and forty years later, The Francis Frith Collection continues in the same innovative tradition and is now one of the foremost publishers of vintage photographs in the world. Some of the current activities include:

INTERIOR DECORATION

Today Frith's photographs can be seen framed and as giant wall murals in thousands of pubs, restaurants, hotels, banks, retail stores and other public buildings throughout the country. In every case they enhance the unique local atmosphere of the places they depict and provide reminders of gentler days in an increasingly busy and frenetic world.

PRODUCT PROMOTIONS

Frith products are used by many major companies to promote the sales of their own products or to reinforce their own history and heritage. Frith promotions have been used by Hovis bread, Courage beers, Scots Porage Oats, Colman's mustard, Cadbury's foods, Mellow Birds coffee, Dunhill pipe tobacco, Guinness, and Bulmer's Cider.

GENEALOGY AND FAMILY HISTORY

As the interest in family history and roots grows world-wide, more and more people are turning to Frith's photographs of Great Britain for images of the towns, villages and streets where their ancestors lived; and, of course, photographs of the churches and chapels where their ancestors were christened, married and buried are an essential part of every genealogy tree and family album.

FRITH PRODUCTS

All Frith photographs are available Framed or just as Mounted Prints and Posters (size 23 x 16 inches). These may be ordered from the address below. Other products available are- Address Books, Calendars, Jigsaws, Canvas Prints, Notelets and local and prestige books.

THE INTERNET

Already ninety thousand Frith photographs can be viewed and purchased on the internet through the Frith websites and a myriad of partner sites.

For more detailed information on Frith companies and products, look at this site:
www.francisfrith.com

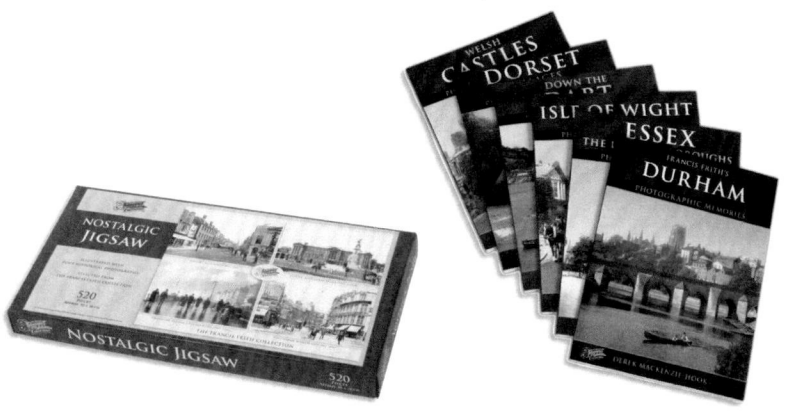

See the complete list of Frith Books at: www.francisfrith.com
This web site is regularly updated with the latest list of publications from The Francis Frith Collection. If you wish to buy books relating to another part of the country that your local bookshop does not stock, you may purchase on-line.

For further information, trade, or author enquiries please contact us at the address below:
The Francis Frith Collection, Unit 6, Oakley Business Park, Wylye Road, Dinton, Wiltshire SP3 5EU.
Tel: +44 (0)1722 716 376   Fax: +44 (0)1722 716 881   Email: sales@francisfrith.co.uk

---

See Frith products on the internet at www.francisfrith.com

FREE PRINT OF YOUR CHOICE

Mounted Print
Overall size 14 x 11 inches (355 x 280mm)

Choose any Frith photograph in this book.
Simply complete the Voucher opposite and return it with your remittance for £3.50 (to cover postage and handling) and we will print the photograph of your choice in SEPIA (size 11 x 8 inches) and supply it in a cream mount with a burgundy rule line (overall size 14 x 11 inches).
Please note: aerial photographs and photographs with a reference number starting with a "Z" are not Frith photographs and cannot be supplied under this offer. Offer valid for delivery to one UK address only.

PLUS: Order additional Mounted Prints at HALF PRICE - £10.00 each (normally £20.00)
If you would like to order more Frith prints from this book, possibly as gifts for friends and family, you can buy them at half price (with no additional postage and handling costs).

PLUS: Have your Mounted Prints framed
For an extra £19.00 per print you can have your mounted print(s) framed in an elegant polished wood and gilt moulding, overall size 16 x 13 inches (no additional postage and handling required).

IMPORTANT!
These special prices are only available if you use this form to order. You must use the ORIGINAL VOUCHER on this page (no copies permitted). We can only despatch to one UK address. This offer cannot be combined with any other offer.

Send completed Voucher form to:
The Francis Frith Collection, Unit 6, Oakley Business Park, Wylye Road, Dinton, Wiltshire SP3 5EU

CHOOSE A PHOTOGRAPH FROM THIS BOOK

Voucher for **FREE** and Reduced Price Frith Prints

Please do not photocopy this voucher. Only the original is valid, so please fill it in, cut it out and return it to us with your order.

Picture ref no	Page no	Qty	Mounted @ £10.00	Framed + £19.00	Total Cost £
		1	Free of charge*	£	£
			£10.00	£	£
			£10.00	£	£
			£10.00	£	£
			£10.00	£	£
			£10.00	£	£

*Please allow 28 days for delivery.
Offer available to one UK address only*

* Post & handling £3.50

Total Order Cost £

Title of this book . . . .
I enclose a cheque/postal order for £ . . . .
made payable to 'The Francis Frith Collection'

OR please debit my Mastercard / Visa / Maestro card, details below

Card Number:

Issue No (Maestro only):   Valid from (Maestro):

Card Security Number: Expires:

Signature:

Name Mr/Mrs/Ms ....

Address ....

....

....

.... Postcode ....

Daytime Tel No ....

Email ....

Valid to 31/12/14

Free Print - see overleaf

Can you help us with information about any of the Frith photographs in this book?

We are gradually compiling an historical record for each of the photographs in the Frith archive. It is always fascinating to find out the names of the people shown in the pictures, as well as insights into the shops, buildings and other features depicted.

If you recognize anyone in the photographs in this book, or if you have information not already included in the author's caption, do let us know. We would love to hear from you, and will try to publish it in future books or articles.

An Invitation from The Francis Frith Collection to Share Your Memories

The 'Share Your Memories' feature of our website allows members of the public to add personal memories relating to the places featured in our photographs, or comment on others already added. Seeing a place from your past can rekindle forgotten or long held memories. Why not visit the website, find photographs of places you know well and add YOUR story for others to read and enjoy? We would love to hear from you!

www.francisfrith.com/memories

Our production team

Frith books are produced by a small dedicated team at offices near Salisbury. Most have worked with the Frith Collection for many years. All have in common one quality: they have a passion for the Frith Collection.

Frith Books and Gifts

We have a wide range of books and gifts available on our website utilising our photographic archive, many of which can be individually personalised.

www.francisfrith.com